THE EAST SIDE OF IT ALL

THE EAST SIDE OF IT ALL

JOSEPH DANDURAND

POEMS

NIGHTWOOD EDITIONS

2020

Nightwood Editions
P.O. Box 1779
Gibsons, BC VON 1VO
Canada
www.nightwoodeditions.com

COVER DESIGN: Charlotte Gray
TYPOGRAPHY: Carleton Wilson
COVER IMAGE: Elinor Atkins

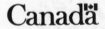

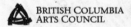

Nightwood Editions acknowledges the support of the Canada Council for the Arts, the
Government of Canada, and the Province of British Columbia through the BC Arts Council.

This book has been produced on 100% post-consumer recycled, ancient-forest-free paper,
processed chlorine-free and printed with vegetable-based dyes.

Printed and bound in Canada.

LIBRARY AND ARCHIVES CANADA CATALOGUING IN PUBLICATION

Title: The east side of it all / by Joseph Dandurand.
Names: Dandurand, Joseph A., author.
Description: Poems
Identifiers: Canadiana (print) 2020021232X | Canadiana (ebook) 20200212338 |
   ISBN 9780889713802 (softcover) | ISBN 9780889713819 (ebook)
Classification: LCC PS8557.A523 E28 2020 | DDC C811/.6—dc23

this book of poems is dedicated to all of the missing

CONTENTS

THIS IS MY PATH

We close our eyes when
a junkie slips by us on
a freshly wetted sidewalk
as the city tries and tries
to wash away the odour
of those who sleep beside
the walls as if they await
entry back into this castle
where all the food is kept.

I have been up and down
the streets of this city
and I never close my eyes
as I wait and accept it all
as the drunk Indian brother
pisses himself, the weak just
keep doing their thing.

I walk on, into the centre
of hell and here I am
greeted with a smile
and she asks me for
a cigarette. I give her
one and she almost walks
away with my lighter.

All I can see in her eyes
are the days of abuse,
the childhood she never
had back home. She looks

at me and smiles knowing
I will never hurt her as we
both blow smoke out
into the centre of hell.

As the sun sets and the moon
rises up into a clear dark
night, the streets move
slower as the day people
lay down for a few hours
of restless sleep and the night
people start their rounds
to search for whatever
it is they need and the
junkies are quick to score
as the dealers lay in wait
for them to change money
for drugs and then the drunks
of the night are already two
bottles in and they puke
it up and continue on as
the working girls and boys
stand on the corners trying
to appear beautiful.
                        To me they are,
as I can see their pasts
and in them I can feel pity
as they get into a truck or
a car to do their thing.

A few hours later
the corner they stand on
is holding them up
as the drugs focus on
their minds and destroy
the horrors of their lives.
As all this is going on,
the moon falls a bit
as the night is almost done
and the sun creeps over
the edge as if watching
the east side and making sure
it is safe enough for the sun
to come out and light
the sorrow
one
more
time.

THE FIRST DAY

When I was five I was put on a bus
and sent to Catholic school
not unlike my mother who was five
when she was put on a train
and sent to residential school,
both feeling that gut feeling
that this was not going to be
a place we would like.

My parents told
my older sister
to watch over me
but she had long ago
grown to not like me,
let alone protect me.

As we waited to go in
that first morning
a group of boys decided
they did not like my brown skin.
The biggest of them came at me
but I was prepared
as I had already been beaten up
when I was four, again
because of the colour of my skin.

So the big kid and I scrapped
and soon the sisters were on us.
We were sent down the hall
as all the other kids
and their glorious uniforms
went down into the classrooms
to begin their first day.
The big kid and I were told
to stand against a brick wall
and the main Sister Superior
of all the sisters told us
if we wished to punch,
then punch the wall.

                              So we did.
As my five-year-old fists
smashed against the wall
and soon blood formed on
my knuckles and the Superior
smiled and praised the Lord.
She told us that was enough
and I kept swinging
as the big boy cried
and said he was sorry. But I wasn't.

The sister again told me to stop
and I threw one more punch
at the wall for her and one more
for Christ who the whole time
stared down from his cross.
And that was the first day
of my time with the Lord.

MUDDY WATERS

The rains wash
the moment away
that I would stop
if I could, to be a
moment of silence
for the ones
we lost this year.

We buried them
across the river.
There they rest
with our ancestors.
Now the river flows
by them and today
the water is
a muddy brown.

We used to place
our dead in cedar boxes
and put them in trees.
The missionaries
made us take them down
and bury them in dirt.

We knew we certainly
did not come from dirt.
The missionaries
would sing songs
from the good book
they carried around

and we would cry
as we covered up another
relation from the sky.

(If we could, we'd dig them up
and lay them in cedar boxes
in a good tree up high.)

Still the muddy waters
flow on as the rains
wash away our tears.
And we burn plates
of their favourite foods
for them. Sometimes
we add a cigarette
or even a can of beer
to quench their thirst.

As we put our brother
to the ground
all the eagles begin
to circle overhead.
We know they are
the ancestors who fell
from the sky. One eagle
dives and takes a fish
from the muddy waters
as the rains fall from
the sky where we
all at one time began.

THE SILENT SCREAM

In the crooks and corners
of the city you see humans bend
over, or they are already bent.
They walk that way down the alley
and some look like snakes
slithering in and out searching
for a white powder or a piece
of black tar. They search and search,
come up for air then dive back down
and bend their spines to the point
of snapping. They do this all day
until they fall over. If we were
to look down from the sky
we would see them left behind,
fallen, as the snake that embodied them
found them no longer worth eating.

There are those who talk
to themselves and we listen
to these great forgotten prophets
as they speak the truth about this
and that and they sometimes scream
to make sure we are listening.
Then they stop for a drink
and continue on as the people
walk by and the prophets smile—
as they know, yes, they know.

We walk on to our lives
and we move in and out from
the hordes who live at each corner
as some sleep and some trade
and deal what they have.
We ignore them and they ignore us
as the streetlight changes from red
to green and we cross over to
another paradise and a new group
and then they bend and preach
and hustle. We ignore them as
we become the snake and we slither
back and forth as we avoid
the dead and the dying
as we search for a better place,
as we search for a better meal.

VIOLINS

As the city sleeps
there are those who
go up and down the alley
picking up whatever may
be laying on the ground
that they toss into carts
and all you hear are
the squeaking wheels
as each cart is pushed
and pushed until it stops
to pick up a pop can
or beer can to toss
into their pile of gold.

They are usually half
the man they used to be.
Some are drunks and
others addicts but they
collect as if collecting
for their choice of church—
God welcomes them all
though some gave up
on God long ago.

There are those who wear
very little and there are those
who are dressed for a cold
winter but here it only rains
and the carts cut through
all the puddles and the half-
a-man stops and picks up
an old needle and checks to see
if it has a drink of the black demon
but it never does so he tosses it
for the next half-a-man to pick up
and repeat as the squeaking wheels
begin to sound like violins
of a pathetic symphony
and the notes are unplugged
in unison as the wheels
turn and stop and repeat.

We all wake up to the early ballad
that is now played with the sounds
of those who cherish a God
as the city becomes alive
from a long night and the song
becomes even louder
as the first bus comes around
and the hiss of the brakes
becomes the drumbeat
and the song changes
and becomes a song to God
who stopped listening long ago.

WAYFINDING

If I were to stop at
every sign I was given
like the sound of an eagle
or the silence and flight
of a young hawk
or growling of a sasquatch
or the jumping fish before my net
or the way the river flows
and the sight of an old crane
as she snaps and kills a fish
with her razor-sharp beak.

If I could, I would turn this
into good medicine
for me and my family
and we would be protected
from all the hate and envy
on this reservation
but I can still hear
the whispers from those
who wait and wait
and take and take
and complain about those of us
who've reset our lives
in a completely different direction.

If we all touched the sky
and asked the questions
we all wanted answered
I would surely ask
what it is like on the other
side and would it be like
this life but much better
and much simpler.

As we all await our final walk
all we can do is listen
and watch for the signs
that will keep us grounded here
and all I can do as the world spins
around and around is watch
for the signs that my life
was always right and my children
have been given enough teachings
not to repeat what I've failed at
and as the day begins,
there are more signs: the call
of the coyote, the shining star,
all of this shown to me
as if I knew what to do with it.

INTO THE CENTRE

One man is up before
the west coast sunrise.
He puts on his shoes
and is out the door,
walks onto the street
and turns left or right
as it still depends on
which way his mind
turns him. He begins
to go straight for the
wicked parts at the
centre of this city
and there he sees
his brothers and
sisters as they
shake or are frozen
in time. He greets
them with a good
morning brother
or sister and they
just stare; they either
smile or just keep fading.

One man arises at night
and he is all by himself
in his room and he puts on
his shoes and is out the door
and goes straight to the centre
and there he gives out cigarettes
to his brothers and sisters.

Some say thank you and others
cannot speak but he does not care.
The night goes on until
the west coast sunrise peeks out
and the man goes back to his room
to light a cigarette for himself,
blows the smoke across
his one-room paradise.

One man is very young
and he puts on his shoes
as he goes out into the world.
He steals what he can and trades
his stolen goods for a small piece
of heroin and he goes to any
hidden place in any hidden alley.
He pulls out his roll of tinfoil
and heats his winnings.
He injects himself and for
a brief time he is still a young man
but that soon disappears
as the high is fading faster,
so he walks back to his room
and lays on his bed as a young man
who has become old. And some day
he will not put on his shoes
but he will stay here, in his room,
an old forgotten man faded away
long before his time.

THE SHAME OF MAN

He is buried somewhere
in a prison of fools. He gets
his meals and a good night's
sleep but he will be gone forever
and most of us do not care
one way or the other
but for our people—
we are the ones who paid
the price as our mothers and sisters
disappeared on his pig farm
a few miles upriver from
where he had taken them.
Now they are just a memory
but we never forget—
as we never forget.

On any given night
they say he would hunt
like all predators downtown
and he'd have his pick
of the already lost and forgotten.
He would pick his target
and bring her back to the farm
where he would keep her
for a few days, feeding her drugs.

Once the desire was
                  too overwhelming
he would attack
                  and explode
                  with his inner demons.
                  He would choose life
                  or death
and in our case
                  it was
                  always death.

With the plunge of the knife
or the cold grasp of his filthy hands
he would end them and
bury them in the back.

As the new day began,
the pigs of the world would feast.

If I could change time
I would wait for the stinking pickup
and that little man in his big boots to appear.
I would follow him and as he picked up my sister,
I would follow him and when he got home upriver,
I would hop the fence and I would get to him
before he could do her any harm and I would
plunge a cold blade into his eye
or I would wrap my hands around his neck
and watch him slip away
and then I would bury him in the back.

My sister and I would return to the city
to await the next predator
and we would do the same.

                But that never happened
and we still search and search for our sisters
as they disappear
and all I can do is stare at my hands
as they strangle an imaginary evil
who still to this day has a nice bed,
a good meal, a lifetime of knowing
he was more than a pig farmer.

STREET SCENE

Early morning and the streets
are alive as the hotels empty
for the night and those lucky
enough to find a room now
begin their walk of shame.

The first thing they need
is a cup of coffee and a smoke.
The streets come to life
as the city day erupts
with the sounds of coughing
and the spitting out
of yesterday's smoke.

A young girl shuffles
to her favourite spot
and tries to stand there
as if she were alive.
The early morning
perverts drive by and
she gets in an old truck.
They turn the corner
and she is gone.
Fifteen minutes later
she is back and lights her
glass pipe, inhales
her lifeline, exhales
the sorrow, then she tries
again to stand straight.
For a moment she appears

like a human, if only
for a moment.

All the elders walk on
to a free breakfast
as if in a race. As they
turn the corner
one lady's in the lead.
The world cheers as
she powers on to the next
turn and then it is uphill
to a breakfast of fresh fruit
and a bowl of mush.
She finishes in first place
as a man in his eighties
comes limping in second
but still happy for a piece
of fruit and some hot mush.

The sirens begin and stop
to revive an addict and he is
now wide-eyed and confused
but high as hell. He smiles
his toothless smile as the street-
lights turn off for the day.
The addict says he is fine
but they carry him off anyway
and he spends the day
in the hospital high as a kite
imagining he is back
home on his reservation
and everyone around him

is his family. He talks to a nurse
as if she were his mother.

She smiles and fixes
the addict's pillow for him.
He keeps talking to his mother
and remembers something
from his childhood. They laugh
then he passes out and
sleeps as the streets outside
explode in the everyday.
The addict dreams about
when he died
                and the world woke him
and now he dreams
of getting back
                to that moment of life,
or death, or both.

STREET HEALER 1

He goes out at night and walks
slowly. They say he fell from
the sky several decades ago
but now he is a fully grown
sasquatch. In the winter
the poor souls gather
round him for warmth
as he hugs them one by one.

He likes to smoke cigars
and does so in his one room
just off the main drag.
As he blows the smoke,
he brushes his long hair
from his face and takes a sip
of cheap wine and stares at
his feet. He smiles, remembering
his mother always telling him
to keep his big feet clean.
So he does as the cigar smoke fills
his one room, his hairy hand raising
one last toast to his mother.

Some nights he meets with the lost
and they ask him for guidance
and forgiveness. He gives them
both, telling them it'll be alright
as they carry on with their misery.
He brushes the hair out of his face
as the next lost brother comes
to show him his wounds. The sasquatch
rubs his hands together and places them
upon the wounds. The man is healed
and says *Thank you* as the sasquatch
turns and pukes out the poison
he has taken from his brother.

One night the sasquatch does not
come out so someone who knows him
goes to his room and finds him
in his final sleep. A cigar in the corner
burns slowly and as the smoke
goes up into the air, the spirit of
this sasquatch also begins to float
back to the sky. As he returns
to his home, he looks back down
to the people of earth
and whispers, *Thank you.*

I DON'T KNOW WHEN I AM GOING

I put a stake into my arm
to become Christ on the cross
and all those thoughts and
big desires come to me
as I take myself off the cross
and my hands and feet bleed.
The blood drips onto the floor
as I sit in this shithole of a city.
For me it is more wonderful
than any picture of heaven.

As the day mixes with torment
and old blessings, I open my eyes.
The first thing I see is the big city
and all the evil. There in the distance
I hear the wolves as they howl
to the great moon. Up into the mountains,
they sip the pure waters and move
even higher to join a group of angels.
Together they dance the night away.

As I sit in my squalor, I remember
being a small child on an island upriver.
We were so simple and all we had to eat
was the fish we caught the last summer.
I remember the salty smoked taste
as my mouthful of new teeth chewed
and chewed. When the drugs are all gone
I know I will be sick so I go out and hunt
for the blackness. When I find it, I stop
and rest and stare up to the heavens.

To me it is just the dark skies
of empty secrets and I smile
as I remember being a child back home.
But now I do not have any teeth
to chew on smoked fish. I stopped
eating long ago anyway and now
inject my liquid dinner into an old arm
and rest here as the heavens open up.
All you can see are the angels and wolves
as they dance upward and upward
until they are no more. The sky
blackens again as I sit here
and chew away what is left of me.

GET AWAY

After roaming the roads,
when I make it back home
there to meet me at my door
is my dog. She wags her tail
and jumps up to ask me about
my adventures. When she settles
down I give her food and water,
then she lies down in her spot.
I go to my room and begin
another journey to get high again.

The lights are always off
and I am as alone as a man
can be. The phone never rings
and no one ever knocks
at my door. The darkness allows me
to flow as the heroin flows.
I am as high as anyone can get
so I light a smoke, swallow
the first drag and blow it out.
But very little comes out.
I take a drink of water and can
barely open my eyes but I do—
and what I see frightens me
so I close my eyes. That too
frightens me so I take another
drag and I almost inhale
the entire smoke. I place
it on a dish that has room
for maybe one more burnt-out

cigarette. I stare at the pile
and enjoy my accomplishment.

I am only about a quarter
of the man I used to be.
Perhaps that is why
the phone never rings
and all my friends and family
let go of me. Now I sit
here with my sleeping dog
and both of us close our eyes
and we dream of the old days
when we ran free and swam
in the river that now flows by us.
We are no longer who we were
as I heat the spoon
kiss the death
welcome the end
forever pity myself
long for a hug
and yes, I even wish
that someone, anyone,
would give me a kiss
as I close my eyes.

TAKE IT SLOW

Out on the river I throw out my net
and drift quietly downriver. The corks
of my net sit, do not bob up and down.
You know there are no longer any fish
left, as man has destroyed another food
and at the end of my drift I begin to pull
in my net. The end begins to dance and
I know it is a spring salmon. It struggles
but I soon get it into my boat. She is a
good-size fish of about eighteen or
nineteen pounds—she will feed my family.
I pull the rest of my net in and turn
my boat around and go back upriver
to the head of our island and again
I throw my net into the river that has
given us life since time began.
Later in the day I try to drop
my net closer to the shore. A fish hits
right away so I race over and it too
looks a good weight, fifteen to eighteen
pounds. I throw it with the first fish
upon a tote of ice. Both look at me
and I thank them for feeding my family.
As I go back to the end of my net,
the other end goes down and I am
caught on a snag. I back my boat
away and try to pull my net off.
I rev my engine and pull and pull
and finally it breaks. I know I have
ripped up my net but I still drift

down and then another fish hits.
I race over and pull it in and that
makes three fish on ice staring at me.
As I pull in my ripped net, I grab
my knife and some twine and find
the break to join the two ends. I mend
them together, cut the end and drop it
back down for the next drift. I sit and
wait and when another fish hits, I race
over, take it out and put it on ice.
I go back to the end of my net and
watch it as we drift back downriver.
This to me is one of those times
in my life that I feel so alive
and I look up and thank the sky
for providing my family fish
for our supper, and others
to put in my freezer for
the long winter ahead.
I look back at my net.
It begins to bob up
and down and again
I join in this dance
of the river:
my net
my knife
my tote of ice
and those eyes
of the fish that give
my family
life.

STREET HEALER 2

She was from a small village
upriver just before the mountains.
She lived here in this city
for the last fifty years,
was known as a healer—
all the folks of the street
would come to her. She would
heal each person the best
she could and they'd thank her
by leaving her something
for her work. She would open
her door for the next one
and as they sat down she'd
rub her hands together,
then place them upon
the person's head and work
her hands down their bodies.
            She would ball up what
she had pulled from them
and blow it out into the air.
She would repeat this
until she had cleansed them.
They'd thank her and leave
something for her work.

When she got older,
she could only see fewer.
Soon they stopped coming,
and she was all alone
sitting there and drinking tea.

She stared at the gifts she'd
been left, waiting for knocks
at the door that never came.
Once she had to go to the hospital
for herself to be cured. When
she returned, someone had
broken in and taken all her gifts.
She sat down, had a cup of tea
and cried as the door stood silent.

The day she died, everyone from
the streets came to pay their respects
for this woman from a small village
upriver just before the mountains.
They cried and sang old songs
and as they wept the healer's spirit
rose up and went into the air.
Everyone saw her as she rubbed
her hands together and blew what
she had gathered one last time,
then disappeared as they sat there
and cried. There was a knock
at the door but no one answered.

PRIZEFIGHTERS

The day when I was four some local
kids decided I was ready for a beating
and they bloodied my lip and I vowed
revenge so I waited for them all to get
off the school bus and I had my hockey
stick ready and I chased them all down
and gave them whacks across the shins.
In the distance I could hear my mother
screaming for me to stop then I walked
back home while the others limped.

In Catholic school on the first day
I was the prizefighter and the sisters
did not cheer me and it was pure hell
from that day forward until I changed
schools and met the prizefighter from
that school and that is when I learned
what it felt like to get punched in the
stomach and as I fell over and almost
puked the prizefighter picked me up
and we have been friends ever since.

In my drunken days I would take on
anyone and win or lose I would get
stronger then I stopped drinking and
just became a fighter and worked all
the downtown seedy bars and would
bounce all the drunks back into the
streets and only got caught a couple
times and went down but got back up
dropped them all with my overhand
right to the temple or jaw and one
night I punched out a patched biker
which was when I decided dying for
ten dollars an hour wasn't worth it.

The only fight I have left is the one in
my head and some days I win and most
I lose and I am humbled by my own self
and today is one of those days where I
square off with my demons and I swing
and swing that amazing overhead right
I sometimes connect so all is good for
this old prizefighter and his hockey stick.

SONGS OF THE MOUNTAINS

There was this man who was
a simple man. He loved his family
and listened to his elders
when they spoke about the past.
Like all of us, this man had a gift.
He could hear songs: he was able
to pull the songs out of the air
when he was on his boat fishing.
He would share them with the elders
and they'd tell him those songs
were gifts and one day they will
go back to where they came from.
But for now, the man was told
to share them in ceremony,
at funerals and gatherings, where
he was joined by drummers
and singers. One day those songs
went back to where they came
from until another young man
had the gift of song.

There was another man they say
came from the sky a thousand
years ago. He had many gifts
but he was very strong and it was
his belief that the people must
listen to his teachings. When they
did not, he would go to them
and give them a choice—and
these men would always

choose wrong. Now they
are turned into large rocks
or mountains. Some were
also punished because they
overfished or hunted too much
or they were just greedy and
selfish. The mountains around
the river grew and grew over
the time he was among us.
He gave us all his teachings
but some of us, even today,
do not listen.

There was this great woman
who carried the gift of love
and she also carried the gift
of giving each child their gift
and she would always travel
by canoe. She would go up and
down the river and she would go
into a village where all the children
came to her and she would touch
each child upon the head and later
in their lives they would find
their gifts. She would also go
to the mothers who had just
given birth where she would kiss
the child and lightly blow into
the child's mouth and each of
these babies would survive
all the diseases our people
would suffer. Each baby would

be given a name and a gift
by this great woman as she
would leave the village
and paddle by canoe upriver.

As she passed by,
a new mountain
would appear
and in the distance
she could hear a song
she had not heard
in a long time.
As she paddled
and paddled,
she smiled.

THE GREAT SNAKE

Our people talked
about a great snake
   that would sometimes
     swim the river
      and would come
       into the village
      where she'd swallow
     all our sick ones
      and when she
       had enough
        of our people
         she'd swim
          downriver
         into the city
          to come out
           of her hole
         at night and slither
        her way down
       each alley
      where the food
     was good
     as she'd
     devour
    the drunkard
    and the addict
   who tasted fine
  and fresh
and no one
ever noticed her
   until the next morning

when the street cleaners
would find the old skin
she had shed
and it would take
four of them
to throw her skin
into the garbage
and the snake
would sleep
the day
with a full belly
and new,
shiny
skin.

Our people talk about how some of our young men had become
wolves and soon were running up and down the river to seek out any
evil man abusing his people and they'd circle this man as he'd weep
for mercy but he'd already destroyed the lives of our young and one
wolf attacked and bit him and as he screamed another wolf attacked
and tore a piece off him until he bled out and all the wolves feasted
upon the evil man and one day they ran into the city and like the
snake they hunted the streets of the city for the evil of man and they
found the men who were hunting our sisters who worked the streets
and the wolves found such a man and they circled him and just when
they were going to attack

the great snake
hissed
as she opened
her mouth
and swallowed
the man
whole
and the
wolves
stopped
and
bowed
their heads
as the snake
went back
into her
hole
as
the evil
man
filled
her belly.

THE LITTLE PEOPLE

In the cedar forests lived
what we called little people.
They inhabited the trees
and when our village slept
they would come in and take
whatever was left outside.
They would find shells
and trade beads
and the odd fishing knife
to take home to the tops
of their great cedar homes.

We'd know when the little people
had been to our village.
We would smile and not
be upset with them—
we'd be upset with ourselves
for leaving anything outside.
And when we would go
into the forest to gather cedar,
at the bottoms of certain trees
we'd sometimes come across
beautiful cedar hats. We'd put
the hats on and continue
to gather cedar and there beneath
another tree would be one
of our fishing knives—
newly sharpened and left
for our fishermen. When we
were done gathering cedar

for the year, we'd leave
fresh fish heads for
the little people, as we knew
they loved fish head soup.

In the winter some years
we would go out into the forest
and start a fire to boil fish heads
for the little people. When we left,
they all came down to sit by
the warmth of the fire as they gorged
themselves on fish head soup.
As we went to sleep, we could
hear the little voices singing songs
of thanks. In the morning we found
cedar hats adorned with seashells
and trade beads and all the trinkets
taken from us a long time before.

LOVE STORY

They'd both have knapsacks
on their backs when they'd walk
the streets to find a good place
to stop and sit and beg for change.
They did well, because they were
so young. He came from a village
on the island and she came
from a village a ways upriver.

At night if they could afford a room
they would lie side by side after
helping each other find a vein
for their magic. They stayed there,
eyes closed, and both went inside
their minds where they'd search
for any happy memory. His would
be when he was a little boy
and his grandfather taught
him how to clean fish and
she would always remember
when she was a little girl
and was given her first puppy.

They both stayed there
as the moon came out
and both stayed there
until the sun came out
and another day of the streets
started all over
for these two lovers.

One cold night they both injected
pure poison that stopped him cold.
She somehow survived
but the damage was done and
she is now in a special hospital
where they feed and care for her
and she just stays there in bed.
When she closes her eyes,
she dreams of the day
she was given her first puppy,
which is all she remembers
as she stays there alone
with her lover no more—
and that is how this love story ends.

FEELING HOLLOW

I have spent many days
in some of the best madhouses.
I'd get so far gone that
I would not eat anymore,
which became like a slow suicide.
So I'd commit myself
just wanting to eat again.
I would begin with some tea
and some dry toast and soon
I'd be on my way back.

I always seemed to get paired
in a room with Christ. He either
liked me or was so far into
the Bible that he saw me as the devil.
He would show me his wounds
and I'd be so deep into torment
that I'd make out where he'd been
nailed to the cross and together
we would pray. On my knees,
I really thought I believed in God
and his good book, though really
I could care less about religion.
But I would drink tea and eat toast
every morning—Christ and I breaking
bread together as his wounds bled.

Down the hallway was a guy
who thought he was a lifeguard.
He would work the hallways and
a couple times I'd seen him save
those who were drowning. Christ
and I watched from our church
down the hall, cheering the lifeguard
as he saved another flailing man—
but we'd all drown eventually
when the water got too deep.

Christ himself died one night
and the next morning they
covered him in white sheets
and took him away. The bed sat
empty until they came and changed
the sheets and it still sat empty
for a few days as I drank more tea
and ate buttered toast as I was
on my way back. Then there was
someone new in the bed beside me
who never said a word. When I
asked him if he wanted to pray,
he opened his eyes, which were as red
as red can be. He just smiled to me—
as I drank tea and ate toast
with peanut butter and honey.

THE STURGEON'S LOVER

In the deepest part of the river
there lived a great sturgeon
and she swam along the bottom
and fed upon the dead who had fallen.
She was about three hundred years old
and when she was full, she came to
the surface and jumped as high as
she could and all the males came
to her and she kissed each male
and let them have her. Months later
she quietly went to her favourite part
of the river and there she released
her eggs in the millions and then began
again to swim the bottom and to search
for any new bodies that had fallen
from upriver, which she feasted upon
with her old softly kissed lips.

The legend goes that a fisherman
had fallen into the waters and was drowning
when the great sturgeon came to him
and asked him for a kiss. He agreed
and the two fell in love and together
they would feed upon all the food
at the bottom of the river. One day
her eggs came to life and created
the people across the water.
The people lived there for centuries
and the sturgeon and man would visit
from time to time, bringing them food

to survive the cold wet winters
until the people too walked into
the water and fell to the bottom
as the man kissed his lover.

Today we do not fish for sturgeon
as their numbers have been decimated
by overfishing and loss of spawning
grounds. Whenever I catch a sturgeon
in my net I let her go and she always
turns back and smiles as she flicks
her mighty tail and splashes me.
My son always laughs as I stand there
stunned and wet, while the great sturgeon
slowly swims away and turns back
to blow us a kiss. We both wipe
our lips as the great sturgeon
falls to the bottom of the water.
There, waiting for her, is her lover.
He kisses her one last time.
She cries as she begins to eat him.

SOMETHING TO GIVE

The man dressed all in black
even on the hottest days of August
walked the streets and would
stop for a free coffee offered
by the many men of the Lord.
He would light a cigarette
and watch the masses scurry
to their next place and then to
the next. He watched the masses
as they hustled a dollar here
and a dollar there. The coffee was
cold, so he turned to a man of God
and thanked him as he took
one more drag of his smoke
and exhaled to the heavens,
or whatever was up there.

The man dressed in black
Walked the streets at night
and would stop at another
mission for another a bowl
of overly salted soup and even
in the muggy heat of August
the soup was very good.
The man sat and watched
the masses as they tried
and tried to get enough
change for a bit of whatever
they'd burn in their glass pipe—
they'd exhale to the heavens,

or whatever was up there.
The soup was finished and
again he thanked the men
of the Lord, then went on
his way as the masses
battled for that one dollar
that had fallen from the sky.

The man lived to be sixty,
but soon began to feel
the effects of being from
the streets. He went for one
more coffee but did not
finish it as he sat and
stared at the masses.
He gently closed his eyes
for the last time. He saw
a great white light,
went to it and began
to float upward. He thought
he was going to heaven,
or whatever was up there.

As he entered eternity,
he dropped his change
back down to the streets—
the masses fought one another
for that one dollar.

AS THE BONES FALL

Along the lower part of the river
all the little Indians were given
time to finally fish for their supper
by the queen and her last colony.
So we went to the river and threw
our nets out and waited for them
to dance the dance and some of us
were lucky enough to catch
our dinner while others struggled
and lost bits and pieces of their nets.
But we have seen this before
and all the while our village
awoke to the mercy of yet
another poor soul being taken
away before her time
from this magnificent world.

At night, our dogs bark to the sound
of a distant train and so do the coyotes.
They all howl together as the train's
horn blasts and blasts. The sky is full
of stars and the moon is only half of
itself. The coyotes go to sleep and
our dogs chase imaginary rabbits,
then they, too, go to sleep.

We eat the fresh fish, fill our bellies
and throw the bones of the first fish
caught to the river. The river says
Thank you as the bones fall and feed
those who live at the bottom
but we cannot fish today because
the queen said so and we gather
to help our family and their loss.
The children all stand and sing goodbye
then we all go home and go to sleep
as the moon is now all of itself.
In the distance a lone coyote
begins to howl and all our dogs
join in. For a moment, it sounds
like a song for our lost.

FROM THE TOP OF THE MOUNTAIN

The sasquatch was raised in
the cedar forest just below
a great mountain that was once
a man who took too many fish—
the man was warned but went ahead
and now he is a beautiful mountain.

The cedar forest was home to all
the sasquatches who lived there
since time began. This sasquatch
decided he would go into the city
and there he put on a long coat
and a pair of sunglasses and walked
every street, sometimes begged
for change, buying a cold beer
and standing with other brothers
on the corner of nowhere.

He became a drunk sasquatch
and all the ladies loved him. He would
go home with them and was quite
the lover but in the end, the ladies
would throw him back to the streets.
He would start over but always ended
up and with his drunken brothers
on another empty corner.

When he was old and broken
and had no more teeth and his
wonderful brown coat was now
a soiled grey, he decided to go back
to the forest where he came from.
There was no one there as everyone
had died from a terrible sickness.

The mountain was still there as he sat
down with his last beer and sipped it
slow. Then he went to sleep one more
time and awoke. He was now a spirit
and decided not to go to the city. No,
he went up the mountain and there
he stayed and watched the world
and all the people fail and fail again.

WHEN THE CITY IS SLEEPING

It felt like the city was fading
and the folks who lived here
were also a shadow of themselves.

It was midday and the sun was out
in full force. All were slowly baking
in their own misery, then a door
opened and a big black crow
walked out with his hair slicked
back. He lit a smoke and walked
onward to a park where all the poor
would gather. The slick crow would
wash away their sins, paid in trinkets
and other stolen goods. The poor
were healed if only for a moment.

The evening brought out another
healer, a wolf with a jean jacket
and hair in a ponytail. She walked
to a corner where all the Indians
gathered and she healed them.
They gave her tobacco and she
went home and rolled a cigarette,
lit it and inhaled the beauty
of those she had healed.

There was a coyote who did not
like anyone. He would steal from
the poor for no reason at all.
Everyone would run away when
they saw him and he would laugh
and howl at them. When he was done
he went home to bed and dreamed
about his family who all died in
a fire set by those he now hunted.

When most of the city was asleep,
the crow and the wolf and the coyote
met up near the river and talked
and laughed and shared their gifts.
The coyote would always take more
than he needed from the bottle of wine
they shared and the crow and the wolf
would laugh at coyote as they all sat
there by the river. In the distance
there is a scream. They look at each
other and smile as the city sleeps.

THERE IS ALWAYS LAUGHTER

Taken back in time by a great storyteller,
I remember the stories as if I were in them
as all the children sat quietly and listened
to the story about a small sasquatch
who grew up to be a kind soul admired
by all the other sasquatches for being so
gentle and soft-spoken. He'd almost died
when a group of hunters came upon his
trail and were outside the cave he'd hidden
in but a wolf and a bear appeared and ate
the men. When the sasquatch came out
days later, the wolf and the bear were gone
and so were the hunters; even their bones
had been taken away by small birds
as the sun rose in the distance.

When I go back in time I remember my mother
would make tea as I would sit and listen to her
tell me about when she was five and put on a train
and was sent to residential school and how she wet
her bed and the sisters made her wear her soiled
sheets for the day as punishment. Mother soon
learned not to tell anyone she'd wet her bed and
as the years went on she learned to be quiet and soft-
spoken and to never tell a soul about the times
the father would abuse her, which she carried into
herself for decades until she was asked for forgiveness
and they forgave her for being a child and today
she falls asleep in the loneliness of still being a child.

Our people struggle but there is always laughter.
This is a gift that will never be taken away nor
will they ever change us. We even laugh at funerals,
laughter covering the pain for yet another lost soul
gone too young and too tragically. The laughter is
ours as we weep and ask why, again, as we bury
our love and all of us go home as a sasquatch
and a wolf and a bear and a child who was put
on a train appear and sit around the fresh dirt.
They do not cry, no, they laugh at it all.

THE GIFT OF FORGIVENESS

In the mountains there lived
a great woman who had the gift
of forgiveness. She would go
to the river people and give
them a reason to carry on. They
needed it when the first big ship
came upriver and nearly wiped
them out with smallpox. She
watched and waited—when
the big ship was gone, she went
to the river people and forgave them.

One hundred and fifty years later,
the river people are still here.
They still suffer but are bringing
back their ceremonies and spiritual
gatherings and no sickness or rules
or laws can stop them. The woman
comes for a visit and they welcome
her and sing songs. They blanket her
and she forgives them. As she
goes back into the mountains,
she is warmed by the blanket
as the people of the river survive.

As the moon rises one night,
the woman of the mountains comes
into the city and meets a young girl
from upriver who tries to survive
the best she can on the streets.
The woman gives the girl a blanket.
As the girl starts to say *Thank you,*
the woman has already left.
The girl walks under the full moon
lighting the streets, then sits down
to wrap the blanket around herself.
She can hear the people of the river
singing songs and closes her eyes
and dreams of her home and family
as the moon opens up the sky
and the woman from the mountains
goes back up to the sky and forgives
each and every one of us.

DAYS INTO DAYS

Days turn into days and hours well they
just creep on and today nothing really
happened, no angels falling and all that
and that poor guy still sits on the cross
in our old church where no one from
our village goes to and kneels and that's
okay too as the day turns into another day.

When you walk with depression
the world can sometimes play tricks
on you and one moment you can crack
a smile and the next your eyes fill with
tears but you fight them off as you are
not ready to sob out loud and that too
is okay, so you try and appear happy
but really your whole being just
wants to scream because life is
sometimes unfair and that poor guy
on the cross he weeps in our old church ·
where we choose not to kneel

For my children I can only imagine
What they are going through after
losing their mother and I am there
for them and they know me pretty
good and we carry on the best we can as
our days become days and the hours fall
as if they were angels from up above.

Let us pray for our children of this
village as the river that surrounds us
spills its tears into the salty ocean
and our children stand up and say
their names and shout out the words
to their mother who is now on the other
side and sometimes they say that God
is there but we have never seen him
and his son sits on a wall in our old
church where we will never kneel.

I LIKE THE ONE

We look for answers—and
they do come in strange dreams
or they are an image you see
when you go out on your boat
to the river and there flying by
are four eagles and they just look
down on you and you look up to
them and then there was that time
you found an eagle feather floating
downriver and you picked it up
and kept it on your boat and that
was the best year of fishing
in a long time and you raised
your hands up the next time
an eagle soared by.

In this life I have seen many things
and have listened to a lot of people
tell me stories about the old times
and these stories are pretty good
and simple. There was that one
about a mink who was quite
the lover and took chances with
the women of others and once
got caught and lost a paw
or was it his tail I cannot
remember but that mink was
quite the lover. I like the one
about sasquatches and how they
appear then are never seen again

and if you ever see one they say
it is good luck and there are even
stories about spirits in the city
like the one I heard about a wolf
becoming a woman who would
walk the streets and help and save
all of our lost people who could
never find their way back home
and she lived to be over
one hundred years old and
when they went to bury her
she had already gone back
to the spirit world and as the last
shovel of dirt was put on her grave
all her friends and the people
she'd saved could hear a wolf
howling and I really liked that story.

WHEN YOU SEE INTO MY EYES

Please save me from the streets
where I have lived the past few
years on and off. I go home from
time to time but the days there
are just as good as the drugs
that find me with a twenty-dollar
bill given to me by my mother
who looks into my eyes for her son
but he is long gone and sits in a one-
room castle where I drive that needle
into my arm and the pleasure is as good
here as it is back on our reservation
about fifty miles upriver from
the piss-stained east side of the city.

Do not try and save me from myself
as they have all tried that before
and I even went to a nice place
on the big island but my stay was short
as I craved more than tea and toast
and words that seemed to be repeated.
There was even a whisper of God
whom I did not know well and they
gave me a big book with stories
and pictures of saints and even
a good drawing of the devil who looked
like another addict I knew, but had passed
a long time ago with the needle still
in his arm, looking a little like
a street-smart Jesus on the wooden cross.

As I light up the poison one last time
I give myself an extra taste to take me
home for the last time and as the liquid
dissolves me I begin to see an opening in
the sky and I go there and to meet me
is my mother who had died a long time
ago and she again stares into my eyes
and this time she can see her son
and then the sky closes and I am swept
away on a river and all around me
are drowning angels and they sing to me
and then I remember a picture from
that old book and then I close my eyes
one more time and then I am gone.

KWANTLEN

If we talked about the past
we would say how strong our people
were and how they had survived
the constant rains and the great floods
and how they lived in the ground
and how they, like us, took the fish
throughout the year and how it fed
their families. And if we talk about
how they would war against other
river and island tribes who would
come upriver to try to take our people
back with them, we would say
we had great warriors who would wait
for their canoes to come to shore
where we would club them to death.

But today we do not use violence
to survive and we have become quiet
and accepting of our neighbours though
in the beginning we were almost wiped out
as sickness came with the people on ships
who wanted to trade and cheat us of our fish.
That sickness nearly wiped out all river people
but today we are still here, and we survive.

Our children have grown up with loss
and alcohol and drugs and they too fight
for their lives in a world that does not
seem to care about them but we try
to teach them the lessons from a long time
before there was anything written down.
In our ceremonies we repeat those words
and our children will also repeat those words
and so we the river people are still here.
We are all the silent warriors and we say
enough is enough and our young they pick up
the drum and they sing new songs
and they stand and shout to the world
that we are still here and will never leave
this simple island on the great river where
we still take the fish and yes, we still live
where we have been for thousands of years
and we are the ancestors of our future as
a child picks up a drum and begins to sing
a new song given to him from long ago.

I WON'T BE AFRAID

A fisherman once told me
he'd seen the most beautiful woman
turn into a giant sturgeon. It is said
today she still swims up and down
the bottom of the river and that she
feeds on the dead. We use this story
to tell our children to respect the river
or the giant woman sturgeon will suck
them up into her giant mouth—some kids
listen and others do not. Even the most
experienced fishermen try their luck
at defying the river and if their net
gets snagged on the bottom
and is taking their boat down,
rather than cut their net they
choose to wait and down
they go to the bottom
where the giant
woman sturgeon
eats well that day.

A story came to me about an owl
who had lived for centuries.
He would show up at funerals
and sit there with his big eyes
staring at all the people who'd come.
When they'd left, he'd fly home
to tell his family of the sorrow
he had seen. His family would
come and hug him, then the owl

would close his eyes and cry.
His tears became the rains
and they would fall on the pile
of fresh dirt where the people
had just buried a love one.

Even in the city I have heard
of a young girl who could talk
to the spirits. She would help
anyone wishing to talk to dead
loved ones and would be given
gifts of blankets. The young girl
would sometimes just sit there
and talk to the spirits for days
as she was so interested in the
old teachings. When she learned
something new she would stand
in the middle of a street to yell it
out and all the people would hear
her and she would stop yelling
and sit down on the ground.
The spirits would come to her
and would share more as the
teaching she had just yelled to
the city was still an echo and
carried on and on and soon
disappeared as it reached the
mountains and even the owl
heard it—and so, too, the giant
woman sturgeon swimming
at the bottom of the river.

WITH A GOOD MIND AND HEART

A raven was talking to me this morning.
He was on the tallest tree on our island
and had a lot to say. I listened for ten
minutes then he was gone. He had left
some good words for me as I struggle
with worry for my children who've
just lost their momma. The raven said
to hold on and be strong and walk
with a good mind and a good heart.

The sky opened up today and I
believe it comes from the other
side and the spirits were letting
me know that she is okay over
there and to tell the kids that
she loves them, so I do. The kids
close their bedroom doors and
I go to my room and curl up
under my blanket.

I shake with fear that there
must be more I can do
so I close my eyes and try
to dream of her but nothing comes
so I open my eyes and know
we are all still crying tears of loss
but that is okay as sorrow is
happiness on the other side
and I know she is happy as
she does not suffer anymore.

In the morning I rise and begin
my routine, as being in a depression
you need routine so I get up and light
a smoke and go get a coffee and light
another smoke and breathe as much
smoke I can breathe and then go back
to our island. As I cross the bridge
the sun comes up on the horizon
and a good song comes on the radio.
I continue my routine and death
and depression love each other.

There is so much to do so I keep
going and check on my kids
and they are still exhausted
so I encourage them to rest but
I know they will walk their walk,
not mine, as their youthfulness
is their greatest gift, keeping me
laughing and seeing me for who
I am and we all go to our rooms
and close the door as the laughter
lifts us higher than the tallest tree
that sat a raven with words of glory.

ONWARD TO THE GREAT RIVER

The streets are where I lay my head
and the buildings are the trees
that I used to know back home
as I sit on the curb and watch all
the characters and some are bent
over as if broken in half to pick at
the ground as if they have dropped
a jewel; some are so high that they
dance as if in a tragic ballet, in such
a wonderful moment it makes me
want to get up and follow and bow
at the end bent over as if broken in half.

There are those who just watch and fix
on me and they watch me as I watch
them and we all look around as the siren
of an ambulance is coming up the road
to recharge an addict who is beyond
this world and the siren stops just up
from where I am sitting and they try
to revive another angel of the streets
but she has already floated into the air,
which the watchers all see, but look
away, and again we stare at each other
wondering who will be next.

The rain is the worst as everything
is soiled and the piss and shit washes
down into the sewers and goes out to
the mighty river and the rains cause me
to stay inside my small room where
I have a bed and a window that stares
at another building. I have to share
a bathroom with others so I sit there
and sip on beer and light a smoke
and sit there and stare out the window
at the next building. I open the window
and can hear another siren and imagine
it to be someone who has been watching
me and I bid them farewell
as the rains stop and you can smell
the shit and piss as it flows onward
to the great river as I close the window
I sip my beer and light another
smoke as I dream of my escape.

TO NOT BELONG

That moment when I was able
to walk through the city and not be
seen, I would walk for days and count
the brothers and sisters as they paused
for a quick fix. Some went for their arms
and others went for their feet and some
went for the neck and all around them
the world moved on and I would sit
beside them as they floated away
into the misery of their high.

I used to sit with drunks in a park
surrounded by pigeons. We'd laugh
and then quietly watch one fight
the other. It never ended well for either,
always a bloody nose or black eye
and we would suck our bottles and
start all over again laughing and crying
and telling stories about our glory days
but they never knew I was there,
and looked right through me as the
next two contenders squared off.

I walked at night and all the predators
would be out hunting their prey who
could not sleep. They'd attack and
waste the youth who were on the street
trying to get some cash for a little taste
for their imaginary glass pipes. I would
watch the tragedy play out and there
was nothing I could do about it because
I did not belong and the prey would
scatter into the darkness of a corner
and they would light up and burn
their minds trying to hide in fear from
the predator who took on the image
of a man hunting the young and
I would watch it all. At the end
of the show I would stand up and
applaud all the people of the night.
Then I would vanish because I did
not belong there in the first place.

THE LAST INDIAN BAR

The rains have stopped and the sun
peeks out and city begins to move as
people gather around to ask the same
question about the fire that burned
down one of the oldest Indian bars,
where they say some of the patrons
were still sitting in their spots
with one hand up to God
and the other on their last beer.

We all knew someone who'd died
in that fire, or we knew someone
who knew someone who had their last
drink in that old bar and the smoke
had not yet settled and even the band
that had been playing some old tunes—
they too stood where they had played
their last note. One survivor,
an old man from upriver who had
stepped out for a smoke, said it all
happened so quickly and it was
like a spirit came in and ignited
the hell from a long time before.

As the last human is taken out
of the gutted bar, the city spirits
went in for one more look.
As they walked around, the spirit
who'd started the fire came in and
the other city spirits recognized her
and quickly ran out as she rubbed
her hands together and blew a breath
into the burnt-out bar. Then she was
gone and all the other spirits were
now running back to their homes.
As they looked back one more time,
the bar disappeared and was
never spoken about again.

WORDS NEVER MENTIONED

Early morning my dog
is growling at grass snakes
that are not even there
but sometimes they are
as they come lie in the sun.
One time my dog grabbed one
and threw it into the air.
The dog felt good about that
then saw a rabbit
and the chase was on.

We should be on the river
but the fish are in trouble
and we may not even be able
to catch one fish for our supper
as the river is closed to us
even into our ten thousandth year
of living here and taking fish
for our supper but we wait for
the queen and her old colony
to give us a chance. Then we
will chase the fish and yes,
the chase will be on.

The sun came out and warmed
all the snakes and the river
which is now a dirty colour
as the snow in the mountains
melts and fills it and we stay
here on this island where
we have been since we fell
from the sky and the sound
of a distant train reminds us
of the colony and the queen
who grows old and not once
did she come see us and share
some smoked fish and no,
she never once uttered
the words *I am sorry.*

My dog has stopped chasing
rabbits that she will never
catch anyway. Now she lays
at my feet as I mend my net
and we stare at my boat
that has yet to see the river
and the horn of a train blasts
the peacefulness of our home
that has been through all
the worries and woes
of our people awaiting
the queen and her colony
to give us a chance to
catch a fish for dinner.

GOING BACK HOME

If she ever went back home
the people would not accept her.

So she stayed in the city,
worked any job she could get.

But it was never enough
to cover her taste of heroin,

so she began to work the corners
of the darkest places on earth.

She'd met all the evil of man—
some left their marks on her.

One day she almost got in a truck
with a pig farmer, but a voice inside

her told her to pass even though her
need to get high was overwhelming.

The man carried on to the next corner
and one of her friends disappeared

forever. Her daughter came to work
the streets like her. Together they survived,

knowing they were not allowed back home.
They take the evil of man and do their best

to live on. Soon they have a baby girl
to care for. They hide the child and bring

her up to be a strong young woman.
One day the young woman walks back

to her village. All the people come out
and welcome her home. She tells them

about her mother and grandmother and
how one day they vanished from the earth.

The people set the table for supper
and the elders tell this young woman

that she will always be from her people.
The young woman cries as the spirits

of her mother and grandmother
arise from the fire that warms us all.

FLIGHT

As the heroin takes me on one more journey I feel like I am cold though I have on a heavy sweater and my feet are dry even as the rains pour down as if unleashed by God himself as he washes his hands of all of us here in the east side of it all. I go to get my wings and they fit perfectly and then I take flight and am beyond the walls that have degraded me since I arrived here. The rains pour as if God himself is trying to drown me again.

As I land back home there is no one there as they all left a long time ago to go back into the sky so I walk around and start a fire and by now the heroin has me in its claws and my mind is not the same one that I had when I left this home and went to the city to find myself and I did—I found the evil man that I was, who would never be loved again—so I open my wings and again fly back to the east side of it all.

When I land and kneel before God he just laughs at me as he allows the sun to come out. The heroin has finished me and as I kneel, my wings fall to the ground and vanish. I am the man that I am and as the sun burns me, the heroin says *Goodbye old friend*, and God looks at me one more time and nods as the sun becomes the heaven that will never welcome me.

SONG OF THE HAWKS

A young hawk whistles at me
and I thank her for the guidance
but soon realize she is not
whistling to me but is singing
a song. So I begin to sing
with her. We are at peace
this early August morning
and we are finally allowed
to fish the river, so I keep
that song in my head
and pray all will go well
and my old boat will run
without problems. I pray
my old net will give me
one fresh fish for dinner
and I sing that song
of the hawk as she glides
away to another tree on
the other side of my life.

That first drift is the most
important one. You pray
the net goes out smoothly,
then shut off your motor.
You watch your net as
you drift, then it begins
to dance in the middle
so you turn on your motor,
release your net and fly
over to where it is dancing

and you pull and pull
until you see the silver
of a fifteen-pound spring
salmon and you lick
your lips and go back to
the end of your net, shut
off your motor and watch
your net as you drift further
down past our village.

In the distance there are now
two hawks. They are each
singing a different song
but soon it becomes one song.
You cry in happiness as you
have a fish to feed your family.

At the end of the day when
the river is closed you head
home, turning the corner
into the slough and along
the shore there are a hundred
hawks. They are all drumming
and singing for you, or so you
think, but they too have caught
a fish and they are actually
singing a song of thanks
to the river. Their song hits you—
you cry again for the river and
for the hawks and you turn
the next corner and can see
your village as the drums

and song are in the distance.
You smile one more time
as a spring salmon jumps
out of the water and looks
you in the eyes, dives back
down and carries her eggs
on her journey up into the
mountains, then releases
them as the song of the
hawks echoes across
the water one last time:
for the fish, for me,
for all of us as we cry.

PHOTO CREDIT: PETER ARKELL

ABOUT THE AUTHOR

Joseph Dandurand is storyteller, poet, playwright and member of Kwantlen First Nation located on the Fraser River about twenty minutes east of Vancouver. He resides there with his three children. Dandurand is the director of the Kwantlen Cultural Centre, artistic director of the Vancouver Poetry House and author of three other books of poetry, *I Want* (Leaf Press, 2015), *Hear and Foretell* (Bookland Press, 2015) and *SH:LAM (The Doctor)* (Mawenzi Press, 2019) and one children's book, *The Sasquatch, the Fire and the Cedar Baskets* (Nightwood Editions, 2020). Dandurand was Vancouver Public Library's 2019 Indigenous storyteller in residence.